FASHION
in the
'30s

JULIAN ROBINSON

FASHION *in the* '30s

ORESKO BOOKS LTD·LONDON

ACKNOWLEDGEMENTS
Sincere thanks are due from the publisher to
the following for permission to reproduce
copyright photographs which appeared in the
editorial pages of the magazines concerned:
Harper's Bazaar, London: photographs on
pages 4/5, 13, 31, 35, 37, 50, 59, 79, 90, 98,
101, 102 and 104;
Femina: photographs on pages 49, 52, 77, 81
and 93;
French *Vogue*: photographs on pages 44, 45,
46, 55, 57 and 80.
The photograph on the title spread is from
Radio Times Hulton Picture Library.

This book is dedicated to my parents for
arranging their lives so that I was fortunate
enough to know the subject of this book at
first hand. To my brothers for helping me to
live through that and the subsequent decades,
and to my children for being so patient whilst
I wrote about what I knew. To you all I am
extremely grateful.

First published in Great Britain by
Oresko Books Ltd., 30 Notting Hill Gate, London WII
Copyright © Oresko Books Ltd. 1978

This edition published by Universal Books Ltd.,
The Grange, Grange Yard, London SE1 3AG
UK ISBN o 905368 44 4 (cloth)

and Park South Books, an imprint of Publishers
Marketing Enterprises Inc. 386, Park Avenue South,
New York, New York 10016
USA ISBN o 917923 10 3

Printed in Spain by Jerez Industrial, S.A.

INTRODUCTION

This book is about the feminine revival and the fashions worn during that glamorous decade, 'The 'thirties', as reported and illustrated in the newspapers and magazines of the period. Since good pictures can convey a message so much better than words, I have decided to place the main emphasis on the original photographs and illustrations, selected from *Harper's Bazaar*, London, *Excelsior Modes*, *Femina*, *La Femme Chic*, *Paris Elégant*, *Très Parisien*, *Journal des Modes*, *The Lady*, French *Vogue*, *L'Officiel*, *Art Goût et Beauté*, American *Vogue*, *Le Miroir des Modes*, *Chic Parisien*, and many others — to all of whom I am deeply indebted.

It is my hope that the pictures chosen and the editorial extracts used will serve as a fitting epitaph to all those couturiers and designers, photographers, illustrators, journalists and editors who helped to make this decade one of the most interesting and glamorous periods of feminine fashion in this or any other century.

Julian Robinson

Lanvin: spangled evening jacket over a pale blue draped dress. Photograph by Baron de Meyer for *Harper's Bazaar*, October 1932.

Maggy Rouff: tweed coat trimmed with leopard. Baron de Meyer's photograph beautifully captures the fashionable look of the early 'thirties.

The NEW FEMININE IMAGE

1930 to 1932

'*Numéro un. Embrasse-moi encore.*' 'Number one. Kiss me again.' The *vendeuse* called out the name and number of the first model of the opening show. It was ten o'clock on a cold, damp Monday morning in late February, yet the salon was packed to bursting. Everyone in the world of fashion was there, for this was the first of the *haute couture* collections to be shown in Paris at the beginning of the new decade. From liner and plane, from all the major cities of the world, important buyers and journalists and the fashionable clientèle had swarmed into the French capital.

Expectancy was in the air. The winter collections of 1929 had been front-page stuff; not for years had designs been so sensational or so revolutionary. The fashionable creators had shown remarkable prescience in staging that revolution; as usual they had tuned into the general trend of events and interpreted it correctly. The dropping of the hem-line and re-introduction of the waistline by both Patou and Chanel had marked the end of an era, one which, however, would be marked in a different way by the Wall Street Crash two months later. Women throughout the western world suddenly realized that they had grown weary of the 'crisp chic' of the late 1920s; they were bored with the standardized vogue for short, tubular dresses, cigarettes in long black holders, cloche hats and bobbed hair. The uniform of the 'bright young things', so sharply portrayed by Noël Coward in *Hay Fever* and his other plays of the period, was outworn.

The woman of 1930 was aware of feeling more attractive, more feminine and more alluring than she had for years. 'Now, thank goodness, women are going to look pretty again', was how one magazine editor reported the news. There were to be no more straight little frocks, no more boyish *gamine* types, all from the same mould. Instead, the fashion world was to rediscover all those subtle curves and graceful lines that are associated with femininity. And what was the 1930s woman going to wear to express this new mood? What new ideas were going to be fashionable? Would the great dressmakers understand her rekindled desires?

By the end of that most strenuous week, when over twenty collections had been shown by the most famous Parisian *maisons de couture,* including Lanvin, Patou, Chanel, Molyneux, Schiaparelli, Augustabernard, Lelong, Vionnet, Worth and the Callot Soeurs, the answers were clear. The new silhouette was very slender and very feminine, designed and cut to follow closely the shape of the figure and moulding the waist and hips. Above, the bodice was slightly bloused, whilst below the hips the dresses widened and flowed softly, often with inset flared panels of very intricate cut. All skirts were longer than the previous spring, reaching mid-way between knee and ankle, whilst some afternoon and evening dresses were ankle-length. One leading magazine described these sensational fashions as 'let loose in the air like a flock of Birds of Paradise that turn and sweep in the sunlight of women's appreciation. All eyes are watching them, seeking the most beautiful styles.' Not surprisingly, there was also an outburst of protest about the enormous costs of such a revolutionary change in those hard economic times, and many editorials slammed the 'Paris Dictators of Fashion'. This attack prompted Baron de Meyer, the leading fashion photographer of the time, to write, 'The responsibility for all new fashions rests with the buyers and private clientèle, with the designer's role being restricted to the suggesting of ideas and novelties with no power to impose, whatever the headlines in officious daily papers say.' And what the buyers and private clientèle had chosen was quite definitely the new, very feminine silhouette.

Chanel's collection, in particular, was a tremendous success, greater even than her revolutionary autumn collection six months earlier. It was universally agreed that this was the best collection that this highly talented French designer had yet produced. It was being talked about everywhere, and the general feeling was that Mlle. Chanel was making exactly the kind of clothes that the fashionable women of London, Paris and New York wanted to wear. She showed evening gowns which were 'picturesque, fanciful and feminine', and day frocks which were 'practical enough to satisfy the country-loving English sportswoman and yet smart enough to please her much travelled American cousins.'

The prestigious Vionnet exhibition marked the end of the Paris dress shows for now, but the respite was short, for soon the mid-season collections would be ready. These were always as competent as the former, but more experimental. Now the *couturiers* tried out 'the long, hip-length, beltless, sweater-like top and wide waistbands', as tentative moves towards lowering the waistline once again. But at the same time they introduced 'very short boleros and very shapely busts', as a recommendation of a higher waistline. Which would their clients like? Did they want short legs and long body, or vice versa? Or did they want to retain the newly established natural waistline and a longer skirt length? These mid-season collections also received sarcastic reviews in the popular press, such as snide remarks about that mysterious creation of the sub-editor's imagination 'Dame Fashion', and renewed complaints about the decrees of the 'Paris Dictators of Fashion'.

However, many women began to realize that it was they themselves who made particular fashions successful. They also realized that the woman who bought her clothes from the great Paris dressmakers did so because she knew them to be artists in their craft, gifted, moreover, with an acute sensibility which enabled them to understand what women wanted — or, perhaps it would be more accurate to say, what women would want next. As artists, they were careful observers of general changes in social life, habits and desires. To quote one leading magazine of the day, 'When women were idle and lived a luxurious life, extreme styles were worn. Today the fashionable woman is so occupied with her work, her social life and with sport and travel that she insists on having clothes which are comfortable and useful. Thus a violent reaction against the excessively short and impractical skirts of the late 1920s was only to be expected.' Nevertheless, some columnists continued to bemoan the dramatic change for several months more.

After the 1930 autumn collections the general impression was that no woman could reasonably complain about lack of diversity in the clothes being offered by the great dressmakers. There were dresses which were distinctly 'jeune fille', and others which were clearly 'grande dame'. Inevitably, some newspaper journalists were very disappointed. They had just seen a number of collections of frocks and gowns developed by the designers on the theme which only a few months before had revolutionized fashion, and which so many of them had bitterly attacked. Now, they complained, there was nothing new, only natural waists, long skirts and wide hems — just what they had been writing about all summer.

Alongside these reports, a new style of fashion journalism was beginning to emerge which reflected in its style the feminine mood it was describing. 'Listen all you who would be smart. I can foretell the autumn styles. Retain a well-developed heart and

Idare: pomegranate red velvet wrap coat trimmed with fox over a white satin dress. The second dress is in soft green panne. Drawing by George Deligne, March 1931.

yards and yards of frilly smiles. These will be favoured as of old, and more becoming you'll admit, while graciousness, rich fold on fold, must show a skin-like perfect fit.' The silhouette of that winter is best described as being for a small-bodied, slender woman with very long legs — a look achieved by imperceptibly raising the waistline and cutting the lengthened skirt in long, unbroken lines. Where there were crossway lines or flounces, they did not run completely around the skirt, so that there was at least one uninterrupted line from waist to hem. Of course, there were deviations from this silhouette, giving, to quote M. Lucien Lelong, one of the great *couturiers* of the period, 'that gaiety, that optimism, that element of surprise and caprice which we now demand of every instant of life.' But it was the long-lined silhouette, entirely modern in its treatment, which was most often worn.

In every department of social life, the war against the geometric designs of the late 'twenties had been waged and finally won. In interior décor, for instance, the gently curved outlines of furniture in the style of Pierre Chareau and Maurice Dufrène had replaced the straight lines of the recently-fashionable glass and metal pieces. Cars, too, reflected the change in emphasis, with the latest models stressing 'real elegance'. Indeed, it was considered of the utmost importance that the car of 1930 should display the latest harmonies of line and colour, for fashion and car design were clearly interlinked. 'Just as dress designers have taken to introducing a bright touch of contrasting colour on a frock or hat', it was noted, 'so the car manufacturers are doing the same, with several exhibits at this year's Motor Show being painted dark green, with turquoise bands, while one superb limousine was chocolate brown and sand colour with lines of burnt orange.' For the élite of society, it was considered the fashion to own the latest eight-cylinder Horch, an English Rolls-Royce, an Italian Isotta Fraschini or the luxurious Hispano-Suiza, especially if the model matched one's smartest winter outfits. One motoring correspondent reported that 'so many of the smartly dressed women who drove up to the exhibition were wearing clothes which exactly matched their cars that one might have been excused for thinking that Clothes and not Cars were the main purpose of the show.'

Jewellery, textiles, ceramics, metalwork and glass had all been affected by this new movement in design. Millinery, of course, also played its part in developing a new kind of elegance. The latest hats were described in lyrical prose as having been 'brought down from heaven on an angel's wing...inspired by the poets...created by some wondrous djinn...' Head-hugging, with a narrow, rolled-back brim, these hats were designed to flatter, provoke, allure, conceal, reveal, tantalize and generally stir up trouble wherever they appeared. So, too, in hairdressing. Gone were the 'Bob' and the 'Eton Crop', to be replaced by smoothly waved hair and tiny curls. Following dress and furnishings, hairdressing had selected the best qualities of the modernist movement. While dress was now very feminine, it was also unfussy; interiors, while well-furnished, made a feature of space. In the same spirit the coiffures of 1930 were never over-burdened. 'The shapely outline of the fashionable head is very feminine, with the "modernist's" ideals of simplicity and proportion being scrupulously observed', best sums up the feeling of the time.

The dress collections the following spring maintained the feminine revival, with fronts in particular being 'au naturel'. In welcoming the return of the natural bust shape, one journalist wrote, 'That lovely curve from shoulder to waist, once woman's proudest possession, has been rescued from oblivion and restored to its natural pride of place. We all remember when to say a figure was "as flat as a board" was to pay one's highest compliment. We cultivated the shoulder hunch and the chin poke, hoping to conceal any lingering curve left after our cucumber-and-pineapple diet had done its worst. We became "boyish"; now, with very much more sense, we are becoming "womanish" once again.'

Vivid colours used in strong contrasts provided another distinguishing feature of these new designs. A year before, harmonies were composed from delicate nuances of one colour, with a bright touch of contrasting colour on hat or frock to create an interesting effect. Now it was thought that much more exciting effects could be obtained by employing several different colours on one outfit, three colours being considered even smarter than two. On the beaches, too, brilliant hues were at last becoming generally accepted. 'Gone are the days when it was part of our insular prudery which prevented attractive beach clothes from being worn around our shores. Gone are the days of the regulation navy-blue serge swimming suit.' That summer the sands were as gay as herbaceous borders, with printed linen play-suits and cretonne beach coats, wide trousers and brightly-coloured sun-shades, bathing caps with colourful rubber flowers, and figure-revealing swimsuits. 'This growing brightness on our beaches is a matter for national rejoicing,' commented one newspaper, 'now that the era of suntan worshipping is upon us.'

The following season, it was announced, women were going to look even taller, thanks to the new autumn fashions shown by the great dressmakers. The Paris salons were full of dresses which gave the look of a long, straight silhouette, although the skirts were not actually straight. Usually they were quite full at the hem, but with the fullness low down and so arranged that it did not break the line. For day wear, this new shape was achieved by pleats, or by a gathered godet inserted low down at the centre back. Panel cutting was also used, being managed with amazing skill so that skirts rippled into the requisite fullness at the hem, with never a pucker to show how it was done. The evening gowns, however, displayed the new style most successfully. These gowns had a simplicity of line and a grace of movement that were considered almost Grecian in spirit; yet they were amazingly intricate, with diagonal sectional seams and crossway panels which 'fitted closely from the waist to just below the hips and then draped about the limbs with an elegant and almost liquid flow, before rippling gracefully to the floor.'

Madeleine Vionnet was without doubt the great expert in this new way of cutting, and her skills were likened to those of a sculptor rather than a dressmaker. There was the 'same regard for the proportions of the human body, the same understanding of the materials in which the work is to be done, as has the sculptor for his stone.' Her bodices and sleeves, for instance, were unlike those of any other dressmaker. She used the whole width of her specially-made, fluid material, and contrived that the sleeves were developed from the bodice without cutting an armhole. Her mastery of fabric was uncanny. She could manipulate seams so that the fabric occurred on the bias over the curved parts of the body, without wrinkles and without gathers. Her secret lay in cut and in using the natural stretch of the material. 'A woman in one of these Vionnet gowns is an expression of the very latest fashion, yet as the eye sees the the supple flow from neck to hem it reminds us of the masterpieces of classic sculpture', was how one writer commented on her work.

Fourrures Max: ermine and Russian sable evening coat. Photograph by Baron de Meyer for *Harper's Bazaar*, September 1931.

Jeanne Lanvin: crêpe-backed silk satin evening dress and fur-trimmed coat. Photograph by Lecram-Vigneau, autumn 1930.

The spring collections of 1932 passed uneventfully. The styles were still very feminine, 'very slim and strict about the hips and waist; beautifully softened around the bosom, the shoulders and the neck.' Skirt lengths stayed more or less where they were, varying just a little according to the type and proportions of the dress.

The summer dresses had a romantic look—but it was remarked that many of those worn at Royal Ascot and the fashionable garden parties lacked the elegance so essential to these occasions. This arose mainly because many women tended to lack critical judgement in their choice of dresses, picking fabrics which were pretty in themselves but which made unbecoming frocks. As one critic wrote, 'They fall in love with a romantic idea instead of taking a clear and critical view of themselves. For a young and pretty girl, the romantic idea in effect might be charming; but it is disastrous for anyone who has lost the ingenuous charm of youth.' Needless to say, this is still the case today.

In the autumn, suits with little jackets were popular, and it seemed likely that women would go on wearing them for some time to come, as they were comfortable and gave the wearer a brisk, youthful air. The most fashionable jacket shape was very short, ending at about the top of the hip bone, and fitting closely into a high waistline. Below this high waist was a slight flare or a shallow basque. For evening, while the accent was still on beautifully-cut dresses with a soft, flowing outline, jewellery acquired a new fashion emphasis. Previously women would select from their cases jewels, a diamond brooch, perhaps, or a pearl necklace, without thinking of them in relation to the gowns that they intended to wear. In 1932, however, it was considered quite improper to mix jewels *ad libitum*. Gowns had to be planned to wear with jewels, and the jewels themselves were given careful consideration. If emeralds were worn, then emeralds alone must be worn. Likewise with diamonds, and if turquoises were to be placed on the ears they should also be worn on the neck and the fingers. Only in the selection of bracelets was the choice not quite so narrow. Here, glittering diamond bands would be permitted to ally themselves with ruby or sapphire ones, provided that they were very discreet, and that they created a subtle harmony with any other stones worn.

This passion for jewellery was one reason for that season's great vogue for the simple black velvet evening gown. Anything more colourful, declared its supporters, would detract from the jewels themselves, just as 'the stars are dimmed by an evening sky, instead of blazing in all their midnight glory.' They were to be as the autumn constellations, one minute 'dark, brooding, full of unguessed-at beauty,' until soon, as 'one by one they begin to shine,' the whole vault of the heavens 'is ablaze against nature's own black velvet.'

Dupouy-Magnin: evening dress in white silk crêpe with matt finish, spring 1931.

Jeanne Lanvin: 'Clair de Lune', a dinner dress in silk lamé from the autumn collection of 1931. Photograph by Scaioni.

Victor Stiebel: evening dress and fur-trimmed jacket from his London spring collection of 1932.

Callot: beige and yellow silk jersey evening dress. Photograph by Henryka Philipp, spring 1932.

READY TO WEAR

Photograph by Shaw Wildman

winter coats with the new slim line

Fur-trimmed . . . deliciously warm . . .

The Hon. Mrs. Bernard found the very coat she wanted—in just her own size—in our READY TO WEAR Department. The photograph will show you that the big curly-lamb collar and the straight slim lines of the coat are distractingly becoming. This tweed can be had in seven lovely colours, and the fur collars come in various smoke greys and browns. It only costs **12½ gns**—and no charge for alterations

Ready-to-wear tweed coat with fur collar available from the Fortnum & Mason Model Room. Advertisement, autumn 1932.

Paquin: model from the spring collection of 1933. Hat
by *Reboux.* Photograph by Dorvyne.

The HOLLYWOOD IMAGE
1933 to 1936

'The great dressmakers would once have denied that the glamorous film star fashions of Hollywood had any influence on the fashions shown in Paris, but it would be untrue for anyone to say so today.' Thus one fashion journalist introduced her readers to the new evening dresses of 1933.

Hollywood had for some time been developing its own glamorous style of fashion in which to clothe its beauties, and in doing so, it began to provide a new inspiration for every woman who took an interest in the latest styles. In the nineteen-twenties and early 'thirties, designers might have conceded that individual stars like Lillian Gish, Theda Bara, Clara Bow, Mary Pickford and Gloria Swanson had had some influence on fashion by introducing an occasional new style into the film-goer's life. 'Once a girl has seen a new style of dress worn successfully by a film star in a picture she is more likely to wear it herself.' However, these stars did not initiate completely new fashions as such. In the mid-1930s, however, the influence of the new Hollywood stars, Greta Garbo, Marlene Dietrich, Tallulah Bankhead, Joan Crawford, Ginger Rogers and Jean Harlow, was undeniable. Of equal, if not greater, importance were the great Hollywood designers Travis Banton and Gilbert Adrian, together with the director Busby Berkeley, who was responsible for many of the glamorous musicals of the period. The Italian designer Schiaparelli was the first of the great Paris *couturiers* to acknowledge this film influence, and she is reported to have said, 'the film fashions of today are your fashions of tomorrow.' The movies dramatized new design ideas for millions of women who had never seen a traditional fashion show. In New York, London or Paris, on a first night in one motion picture theatre alone, ten times as many people saw a new design launched than ever witnessed such a launching at a Paris salon.

But was this new, film star glamour really synonymous with fashion? Here we can look back to the formula first introduced by the great nineteenth-century *couturier* Charles Worth, who wrote, ' the secret of being fashionable lies in knowing where to stick out and where not to.' If this was still the criterion, there can be little doubt that the Hollywood stars of the 'thirties knew all they needed to about fashion. Day clothes in 1933 were as stylish as evening gowns were glamorous. The emphasis of the new silhouette was on the shoulders, with some jutting out in military style with bold epaulettes. 'If you draw a square balanced on top of a narrow oblong you will get an idea of this ultra-smart silhouette,' wrote one journalist. 'The top of the square should be in line with the shoulders; the lower part cutting across the figure at elbow level with the oblong representing the long, narrow, tubular line of the skirt.' Schiaparelli mastered this exaggerated, military silhouette superbly, and it was her designs that were the most stunning.

In the autumn, Schiaparelli's square-shouldered silhouette reappeared, though in a slightly less exaggerated form. But, as often happens in the world of fashion design, 'one idea always leads to another, and no sooner is a new mode fairly launched than all sorts of variations begin to spring up like mushrooms on a warm autumn evening. One by one new points of interest come up — fresh experiments, new ways of doing things—while ideas that no one had entertained before appear to spring, simultaneously, to many minds.' Thus another variation of the ultra-smart silhouette was born in Paris, aimed at what every fashionable woman now sought above all else in 1933, 'glamour', Hollywood-style.

The evening clothes that autumn also reflected a return to the financial stability which had been so badly shaken in the Wall Street crash and the subsequent industrial slump. By September it seemed that prosperity was returning: there were reports of more employment for both men and women, more dividends were being paid by industry, and the stock market was showing such a pleasant buoyancy that little fortunes were once again being reaped — ones which would inevitably be spent. In Paris, as if to emphasize this renewed confidence, gold was used in abundance; 'there were whole dresses of gold lamé and moiré dresses shot with gold; evening coats of ciré satin sprayed with eighteen-carat gold; head-dresses with gold necklaces and bold bracelets of gold to match a simple velvet gown ... woollen materials used for coats and suits had bold gold checks and jersey material used for dresses was woven like gold chain-mail ... in fact there seems to be a veritable gold fever.' Other reports emphasized the use of expensive furs, rich, heavy silks, jewel-studded belts, *passementerie* with sequins and flashing *paillettes*, and velvet in glowing colours. The long, cold winter of 1933 was certainly a sumptuous one.

In the spring of 1934 the age of elastication was announced by headlines that stretched across the pages of the latest fashion magazines. Undoubtedly the most epoch-making event of the year, from the fashion point of view, was the appearance of the new elasticated fabric which enabled dresses to be made without fastenings, and the inventive Mme. Schiaparelli showed a whole series of garments in the new American Lastex material. These stretch fabrics ranged widely from a crinkled, crêpe-like tweed in big checks to a fine ciré jersey, with the Lastex yarn being used as an integral part of the fabric design. Schiaparelli's novelty hats also added interest to that spring, the most admired being those perched high and forward, with long, shaggy tassels.

Most of the other designers continued to make 'the most glamorous, most becoming clothes you have ever seen in any of your wildest dreams.' Vionnet, 'the queen of the fluid cut, the empress of distinction', was praised for 'her new silhouette that is romance personified with its billowy sleeves and skin-tight lines, which make you feel irresistible.' 'Do you desire to "swank"?' women were asked, 'Do you incline towards the richness of furs? ... Do you like feeling as sumptuous as a modern Borgia? — Lanvin does it and adds all you lack ... Chanel loves gold and Lelong transforms you into a complete ingot of that precious molten material.' 'As for the new, fashionable nudity, bishops must resign themselves to it, as anyone wearing the newest evening dresses will be much more naked this summer ... Mainbocher puts nothing above the waistline but boned-up points just covering the bust ... Lelong gashes the fronts of his dresses almost to the waist ... Schiaparelli calls attention to the swell of the breasts by cutting the tops of her dresses a little lower than anyone else dares ... whilst Augustabernard's gowns seem even more naked than the latest scanty bathing suits.' Only a frill and a few lace flowers, it would appear, rescued the wearers from complete immodesty.

Parisian *haute couture* offered the world a little 'Romanticism' that winter, 'not a staggering dose of it, for we can never forget that we are living in the Machine Age', but enough to send several leading journalists into lush prose. There were Schiaparelli's spectacular capes in shaggy lamé fur, Molyneux's streamlined silhouette in brilliant crêpes, Augustabernard's superb sequined jackets, Alix's marvellous quilted ciré satin coats brushed with gold, Lelong's dramatic moiréd capes faced with mink, and many

Reboux: Paris spring hats. Featured in *Excelsior Modes,* March 1933. Photographs by Lipnitzki.

Jeanne Lanvin: 'Mistral', a blue and white checked wool suit with wheat-coloured beret; and 'L'été dans le parc', a blue crêpe dress with sleeves in English lace and cummerbund in bright red taffeta. Photographs by Lipnitzki, spring 1933.

other extravagantly beautiful materials, all of which required the wearer to adopt a grand manner with a 'despise-the-ground-you-walk-on attitude, as if you were an Infanta of Spain'. The buyers, journalists and private clients sat through these fairytale collections, 'half dreaming they were at a Story Book Ball', while the Vionnet collection was considered 'the stuff that romantic dreams were made from'. And when the shows were finally over, when the floors that were once gay with the swirl of chiffon skirts, the sheen of silk stockings and the tap of satin shoes, were deserted, and when the mannequins had vanished with the shimmer of their sequined cloaks, only their perfumes lingered on to echo the beauty that had passed by — 'Dans la Nuit', 'Que Sais-je', 'Adieu Sagesse' and 'Il Pleut des Baisers' — ghosts of a thousand memories, 'that will for ever be revived in their fragrance'.

Both perfume and cosmetics were big fashion news that year. According to one American advertisement, 'Cleopatra didn't just dab a little essence of violets behind her ears. Instead she used rare perfumes in greater quantity than any woman before or since... The use of aromatics and facial decoration dates from the very dawn of history. From the very earliest days, man began to bend nature to his services and to draw from her secret resources. Down from the days of the Pharaohs, royal personages and the gilded youth of their courts lavishly used all manner of precious perfumes, unguents and powders.' In the Middle Ages, the advertisement continued, perfumery became a fine art in the courts of Europe for the use of 'the ladies and the fine elegants'. In 1934, however, the *couturier* was the alchemist, and no dress collection was complete without its new 'Amour-Amour' or 'Number 5', and no lady of fashion in France or America was complete without the new season's rouge, lipstick and perfume.

England was apparently slower at mastering the use of these aids to loveliness. According to a leading beauty magazine of the period, not only were most Englishwomen mere amateurs at 'the game', but they didn't even enjoy it. It would seem that they were still hesitant about the use of artificial beauty aids, preferring simplicity to subtlety in their toilet. However, by the end of the year the big breakthrough came, mainly owing to the continued efforts of the American publicity machine which marketed the glamour and sex-appeal of make-up and perfume as essential ingredients of modern fashion — as, indeed, they now were. As one publicity story put it, 'Once upon a time, there were ladies who were beautiful... "really beautiful"... with Grecian noses, flawless features, swanlike necks and peaches-and-cream complexions — and everybody admired and loved them and gave them presents, and princes married them whenever possible. There were also ugly ducklings who seemed to have had a very bad time indeed. But now, with modern cosmetics specially invented for the Hollywood Stars, everything is different.'

By the middle of the 'thirties, every fashionable woman knew that 'face powder and rouge, scientifically blended and with balanced chromatic colouring', produced a satin-smooth effect on the most uneven skin; that moisture-proof lipstick reshaped the mouth and made the lips glow; that rouge added colour and life to the cheeks; that eyebrow pencil gave the brows pronounced shape and heightened colouring, giving them a soft sheen; that eye shadow added depth and expressiveness; that eyelash make-up made lashes appear longer and heavier and brought out the fine colouring of the eyes. Everybody was asked to notice the rare beauty of the great Hollywood stars who had been helped to 'blaze to stardom', by the use of these cosmetics, for every woman could capture the new Hollywood-style glamour for everyone else to admire.

Lingerie was also greatly influenced by the stars of the screen, and the woman in the street was offered the opportunity to be equally alluring in silk and lace underclothes, described as 'nothing more than a mere whisp of fabric protecting your feminine modesty'. On screen, the wearing of these scantily cut and seductively trimmed nothingnesses was banned in 1934 under the Hays Office Code of Film Production. There was no ban, however, on the 'glamour girls of filmland' letting their fans see how they relaxed at home, and they were pictured, in the pages of the popular weekly movie magazines and the occasional glossy, in the season's silk and lace negligées or pastel-coloured, silk crêpe-de-chine camiknickers and matching slips.

At the beginning of 1935 the world of high fashion was stunned by the 'sparkling, gay and light-hearted clothes shown in the Spring Collections of the great French Couture Houses'. Not since the beginning of the decade had Paris shown so many original ideas using drapery, an intricate technique which demanded all the expertise of the great *haute couture* dressmakers. At Marcel Rochas there were magnificently draped dresses with panels sweeping from shoulder to floor; Lanvin's drapery fell 'like the majestic portières of an Oriental palace.' Schiaparelli's draped and swathed dresses transformed her mannequins into eastern princesses. Alix's dresses were even more oriental in style, with gold- bordered gauzes wound round her models, saris thrown over their heads, and on their feet absolutely flat Dervish sandals. More surprises came with Mainbocher's Turkish trousers with underbloused hems. Wired, swirling and undulating hems were also being shown, and pleated skirts came swinging and swishing back for day wear at Lelong and Molyneux. And everywhere in Paris there was a riot of fabric flowers and floral prints, enough to make any real flowers in the vicinity curl up and die of envy.

In London, too, excitement was in the air — the same kind of excitement felt at a fashionable first night. Photographers crowded into the salons, as at a new Cochran production. The shows themselves were full of 'lovely smiling girls, correctly equipped from hat to shoe, who wore the clothes so naturally that every woman in the audience could imagine herself dressed in the same way.' The reason for this marked improvement in London *couture* was that the London fashions were now being sought out by the smartest American women, who had decided that 'the British well-bred carelessness, cultivated by impeccable tailoring' was just right for their newly-acquired international fashion image. The London *couturiers* also designed special clothes for the London season which was, of course, the main topic of conversation at society gatherings. For the English débutante, the crowning event of the year, next to her wedding, was her Presentation at Court. Court gowns required a certain luxuriousness and grandeur to stand out among the elaborately braided uniforms, gilded furniture and gorgeous decorations of the State Rooms at Buckingham Palace. Rich brocades and satins were essential, with bugles, pearls, sequins, diamanté and jewelled trimmings being lavishly used. Happily, these styles were the forte of the London *couturiers,* and now that débutantes were no longer restricted to white, as previously dictated by Court etiquette, the sparkle of pale blue, lemon and pink could be seen in all of the most fashionable work-rooms in and around Grosvenor Street and Berkeley Square.

Away from such formal occasions, dogs played a rôle in the fashions of 1935. Thus,

SPRING GREEN & WHITE . . . .

ready to wear

Photograph by Shaw Wildman.

Mrs. Philip Kindersley looks deliciously cool and utterly Spring - like in one of our newest Ready-to-Wear suits. The material is a fine open-weave wool tweed in pale green, and the white piqué revers are distinctly 1933. We stock this suit in a large range of colours and four different sizes. Price 8½ gns.

The hat of fine smooth straw is a Marie Christiane model that we copy to your order in our hat department.

Ready-to-wear spring suit in pale green tweed with piqué collar from Fortnum & Mason. Advertisement, May 1933.

if you had acquired 'a slim navy suit and white tailored blouse, the dog on your lead should most assuredly be an enormous spotted dalmation ... Grey flannel needs a blue chow ... Lovely little blondes, a few feathery golden pekes ... The tall and slender are well advised to be accompanied by a huge Irish wolfhound ... Whilst a golden retriever or cocker spaniel is said to make brown tweeds look their best.'

During the summer the journey between Europe and North America became a little easier and a great deal more glamorous with the introduction into regular service of the *Normandie.* This great French liner made her maiden voyage in June, exceeding the highest expectations. The cabins were luxurious, the halls and restaurants elegant, the salons were magnificent and the state rooms sumptuous, 'all gold and glittering, like imagined rooms in a Babylonian Palace.' The *Normandie* had been conceived and designed as a superb floating showcase for the great French decorative artists of the day. There were glass panels by René Lalique, lacquered decorations by Jean Dunand, gilded furniture by Goudissart, bronzes by Dejean, metal panels by Raymond Subes, velour drapes by Colcombet, bas-reliefs by Janniot, and a complete salon by Emile-Jacques Ruhlmann. That autumn, the buyers descended on Paris once again — from America on the *Normandie,* and from London by the new Imperial Airways' Heracles. Bosoms, they soon discovered, were once again the main focus of fashion attention, although there was by no means complete consistency in this new mode. Indeed, 'fashion begins where consistency leaves off' seems to have been the message that autumn, and no one could have accused the fashion world of having been monotonous that season. Editorials suggested that to be 'really smart' you should wear 'Talbot's outrageous gnome's hat, velvet-edged in a crackly white cellophane scroll', that you should stun your friends 'by concealing yourself in the sensational silver fox cape by Molyneux, tapered from top to toe', or that you could go completely berserk and try Schiaparelli's white plaster mask with red feathered eyelashes, with black gloves with scarlet finger nails; and rather than an every-day hat, you could place on your head 'one of those Surrealist-inspired, crazy little gadgets'.

The Transatlantic, typically aggressive journalism was used to the full that autumn. 'Paris Dress Sensation!' and 'Fashion or Farce?' screamed the huge headlines of English and American national and provincial newspapers. The use of such shock tactics became increasingly evident as the decade progressed, the general philosophy being 'the wilder the whim the larger the print'. The fashions themselves became lost in this sensationalism, which concentrated on the unusual and curious. Many of the fashion reports of this period must have read like stories of mystery and horror in which, whilst the reader's blood curdled at the lurid details, she could, if she was lucky, pick up one or two clues as to what was really going on; it was difficult, though, to discover how clothes were really supposed to look. Advertising, too, was notable for its lack of subtlety. From the pages of the glossy magazines the reader was harangued, 'Foul creatures, your teeth are dirty, your gums are poisoned, your breath is bad, your very bodies stink. And as for your hair, it's falling out or growing in the wrong places. You're spotty, too, and you don't even wash your undies properly.' Owing to their disgusting habits, the readers' children were ashamed of them, their lovers avoided them and their neighbours laughed at them. Finally, these miserable wretches were offered the opportunity to become fit members of civilized society by investing in the latest toothpaste, soap, talcum powder, or whatever beauty aid was being advertised.

In the spring of 1936, flowers were once again at the centre of fashion interest, with 'luxuriant blooms running riot all over very pale or very dark grounds; carnations, lilies, large daisies or hemlock and roses; some in silhouette on long tapering stems like Chinese paintings, whilst others are printed in the colours of an herbaceous border.' Hats, too, were bursting into bloom with 'such astonishingly real looking flowers that bees might be seen buzzing round them.' The more extreme versions were 'reminiscent of an overgrown greenhouse — just like those we used to joke about last year, only we daren't say so any more.'

In the autumn, Exits became just as important as Entrances, with the back view of one's outfit attracting all the attention. The back of a tailored suit was prominent with pleated peplums and folded panels, whilst at night almost anything could happen behind your back. Rhinestone buttons might highlight the spinal column; bustle effects added fullness, as did panels of fluted frills with gathered insets — all of which must have made standing up very impressive but sitting down rather precarious. Even the high-crowned hats were decorated from behind, so that you would have needed eyes in the back of your head to appreciate your new appearance properly.

As for furs, there was a lot of masquerading going on, which threw the traditional taxidermist's ideas to the wind. Opossum was dyed bright red, astrakhan dyed bright blue, caracul and baby goat dyed and used like tweed; monkey fur was also being used in ways nature never intended. But the fur of the autumn season was undoubtedly silver fox, for round, soft coats, wrist-length and warm, and which gave a bulky look to the top of the silhouette, contrasting with the sylphic appearance below. Capes, too, were best made in silver fox, 'particularly those made from pelts mounted vertically on chiffon or crêpe with a breathing space left between each'.

However, the highlights of the fashions that year — at least as far as the press was concerned — were Surrealistic in influence. There were reports of white eyelids and green eyelashes, blue finger-nails and mauve toe-nails, an evening dress with a larger than life-sized red lobster print, buttons resembling anything from a crab's claw to fighting monkeys, extreme evening hats reminiscent of bird-cages, and of course the famous Schiaparelli-Dali black felt hat in the shape of a shoe, with its shocking pink velvet heel. 'What next?' demanded an indignant reporter. 'Shoes in the shape of hats, I suppose.'

He was wrong, though. The next theme to dominate new designs was not the 'shock appeal' of Surrealism but the more down-to-earth theme of Sex Appeal.

BEACH FASHIONS GO FEMININE..

skirts are skirts in 1933

Tremendously becoming are the new beach frocks we have designed for you this year. A lovely silk canvas material patterned in red and white, makes this model worn by Miss Diana Gould, one of our leading young dancers who is making a big success in "Atalanta" at the Ballet Club. The dress is backless, has a long swathed sash that ties at the back, and the flared skirt is amusingly slit up to show your proudly tanned legs

From our Model Room, 1st floor

Photograph by Shaw Wildman

Long beach dress from the Fortnum & Mason summer range, 1933.

Illustrator Reynaldo Luza's swimming pool on the Mediterranean. Photograph by Jean Moral for *Harper's Bazaar*, July 1933.

Molyneux: autumn tweed suits. Featured in *Excelsior Modes,* September 1933. Photograph by Lipnitzki.

Paquin: afternoon dress and coat with asymmetrical fur trimming. Photograph by Scaioni, autumn 1933.

Chanel: double-breasted worsted suit with white hand-kerchief linen blouse. Grey felt hat banded with navy by *Rose Descat*. Photograph by Luza-Moral for *Harper's Bazaar*, September 1933.

◄

Alix: 'oriental' draped silk crêpe dress for the autumn collection of 1933. Photograph by Georges Saad.

Jodelle: soft wool street dress and fur cape. Hat with veil by *Rose Valois*. Photograph by Georges Saad, October 1933.

William Ogden: advertisement for jewellery. Photograph
by Scaioni, December 1933.

Hartnell: evening ensemble in ivory satin glittering
with gold paillettes. Photograph by Luza-Gutmann for
Harper's Bazaar, April 1934.

English golfing outfit by Leathercraft, photographed against the new Alvis Sixteen. Advertisement, June 1934.

Matita: travelling ensemble in cream and brown tweed, photographed against The Royal Highlander. Advertisement, autumn 1934.

39

Rose Valois: autumn hats from the Paris collection of
September 1934. Photographs by Dorvyne.

Lucienne: feather-trimmed hat from the Paris autumn collection of 1934. Photograph by Georges Saad.

Liberty's evening gown in black ciré chiffon with feather-trimmed cape, from their ready-to-wear collection, autumn 1934.

Jeanne Lanvin: grand evening dress in white silk with paillette bodice. Photograph by Dorvyne, September 1934.

Chanel: flowered organdie evening dress. Photograph by Lipnitzki, October 1934.

Lucien Lelong: evening ensemble from the winter collection of 1934. Photograph by Georges Saad, October 1934.

Jodelle: winter coat in grey wool with side fastening of crystal buttons and fur collar. Featured in French *Vogue,* October 1934.

Alix: evening coat in silk ciré. Photograph by Hoyningen-Huène for French *Vogue,* October 1934.

Augustabernard: dinner dress in grey silk crêpe. Jewels by *Boucheron*. Photograph by Hoyningen-Huène for French *Vogue,* October 1934.

Schiaparelli: draped wool afternoon dress from the winter collection of 1934. Photograph by Scaioni.

Maggy Rouff: white velour d'Albène evening dress from the winter collection of 1934. Photograph by Dorvyne.

Jean Patou: evening dress and cape in tiers of blue organdie, with two large clematis in pale mauve organza. Photograph by Georges Saad, October 1934.

Schiaparelli: Rayon evening dress from the winter collection of 1934. Photograph by Georges Saad.

Reboux: hat with spring swallows. Photograph by Paul O'Doyé for *Femina,* February 1935.

Maggy Rouff: dress and jacket ensembles for travelling. Photograph by Lipnitzki for *Femina,* February 1935.

Weatherill: Katharine Hepburn in grey flannel and gabardine trouser suit with white wool scarf. Photograph by Munkacsi for *Harper's Bazaar,* February 1935.

Maggy Rouff: resort mix-and-match casuals in jersey d'Albène and the new textile 'Peau d'Eve' by Thiébault-Brion from the spring collection of 1935 Photograph by Dorvyne, March 1935.

Hubert, Renée Suzanne and *Dupouy:* silk evening dresses from the spring collections of 1934. Design for *Paris Elégant,* May 1934.

Mainbocher: touring cape and dress in tulle of mixed black, white and green wool. Photograph by Lipnitzki for *Femina,* February 1935.

Zimmermann and *Estelle:* softly tailored suit and three-quarter length coats from the mid-season spring collections of 1935.

Lucien Lelong: draped silk crêpe dinner dresses from the spring collection of 1935. Photograph by Horst for French *Vogue*, April 1935.

Lucien Lelong: printed silk dress and white organdie cape. Photograph by Georges Saad, March 1935.

Alix: draped jersey d'Albène dinner dress. Photograph by Horst for French *Vogue,* April 1935.

Paquin: long afternoon dress in azure Chantilly lace on a blue tulle background from the spring collection of 1935. Photograph by Georges Saad for *Excelsior Modes.*

Madeleine Vionnet: silk afternoon dress. Straw hat by *Reboux.* Photograph by Georges Saad, April 1935.

Marcel Rochas: white evening dress and bolero with sash and flowers in blue. Photograph by Georges Saad for *Excelsior Modes,* May 1935.

A fashionable publicity party featuring dresses from the London spring collections of 1935. Action photograph by Hoyningen-Huène for *Harper's Bazaar*, May 1935.

Matita: 'bon voyage' ready-to-wear wool dress and coat. Advertisement, May 1935.

Coiffure by *Guillaume*, gown by *Vionnet*, with ear-rings
by *Van Cleef and Arpels*, May 1935.

Alexandrine: leather accessories. Advertisement, May 1935.

Maurèse: gowns for Royal Ascot available from Brompton Road, London. Advertisement, May 1935.

Molyneux and *Schiaparelli:* resort casuals. Photographs by Dorvyne and Georges Saad, May 1935.

Hermès: Parisian beachwear. Photographs by Georges Saad, May 1935.

Schiaparelli: printed silk transformation dress. Photograph by Scaioni, May 1935.

Jean Harlow in a Metro-Goldwyn publicity photograph, June 1935.

Hats for Ascot from Debenham & Freebody. Advertisement, June 1935.

Hartnell: classically cut dusty grey Parma violet evening ensemble, in dull crêpe contrasting with a glimmering coat of mail. Advertisement, July 1935.

Lucien Lelong: after-six ensemble with deep fringing from the autumn collection of 1935.

Molyneux: feathered hat and black silk satin dress.
Photograph by Georges Saad, October 1935.

Robert Piguet: classically draped evening dress from the winter collection of 1935. Photograph by Dorvyne, October 1935.

Jean Patou: tailored silk satin evening suit. Photograph by Georges Saad, October 1935.

Schiaparelli: tailored black wool autumn suit with fur cuffs. Photograph by Anzon for *Excelsior Modes,* October 1935.

Jodelle: autumn ensemble in black wool and fox fur. Hat by *Rose Valois*. Photograph by Georges Saad, October 1935.

Maggy Rouff: dinner and cabaret ensemble in black velvet with fox fur trimming. Hat by *Le Monnier*. Photograph by Georges Saad for *Excelsior Modes*, October 1935.

Paquin: winter fur coat in Persian lamb, with *Schiaparelli's* muff and cap. *Lanvin:* broadtail coat and muff. Drawing by Gaston Sudaka, October 1936.

Marcel Rochas: fringed black wool dress and cape from the winter collection of 1935. Photograph by Dorvyne, October 1935.

Marcel Rochas: holiday and yachting clothes designed for a Mediterranean cruise. Drawing by Pierre Mourgue, June 1935.

Nina Ricci: brick red fur-trimmed wool suit from the autumn collection of 1937. Drawing by Pierre Mourgue, October 1937.

Reboux: feather-trimmed lamé evening hat. Photograph by Lipnitzki, November 1935.

Madeleine Vionnet: white moiréd lamé evening dress with rouleau decoration. Photograph by Georges Saad, October 1935.

Lucien Lelong: silk crêpe evening dress. Photograph by **Georges Saad, November 1935**.

Lucienne: novelty golfing outfit. Hats by *Reboux*.
Photograph by Lipnitzki, November 1935.

Alix: white velvet evening coat and blue velvet dress.
Photograph by Lipnitzki, December 1935.

Bernard Newman: Ginger Rogers's wardrobe for her Hollywood film *In Person*, January 1936.

O'Rossen: tailored suit. Photograph by Lipnitzki in a mid-'thirties interior featured in *Femina,* March 1936.

This advertisement reflects the 'glamour' of Marlene Dietrich's legs, so widely publicized during the mid-'thirties. *Harper's Bazaar,* June 1935.

Schiaparelli: design for Helen Vinson in the Gaumont British film *The Tunnel,* March 1936.

Below. Mary Brian wears this smart natural coloured tweed suit flecked with brown in her new film "Two's Company." Blouse, gloves, belt and hat are of nigger brown, and an orange feather mount decorates the hat.

Far Left. There is a delightful Edwardian air about this afternoon gown of filmy white net trimmed with rows of ruching with its modified "leg o' mutton" sleeves, and its tight fitting skirt which finishes in "bouffance" from knee to hem. It is worn by Antoinette Cellier, the British screen actress in her new film "The Tenth Man."

Below. Jean Harlow chooses for formal evening occasions this gown of pleated white georgette. Devoid of any trimming its effect is obtained by beauty of line.

Above. Ice blue satin studded with silver nail head trimming fashions this lovely evening gown worn by Virginia Bruce.

12

Film fashions of 1936 modelled by Mary Brian, Virginia Bruce, Antoinette Cellier and Jean Harlow, August 1936.

Heim: pale blue crêpe evening dress with 'Grecian' pleated drapery. Photograph by Man Ray for *Harper's Bazaar*, July 1936.

Suzanne Talbot: autumn hat in heavy black faille with a bow and parted chenille veil. Photograph by Lipnitzki for *Femina,* September 1936.

Robert Piguet: velvet dinner suit. Hat by *Boy.* Photograph by André Durst for French *Vogue,* October 1936.

Andrébrun: winter astrakhan fur coat. Advertisement, October 1936.

Albert Hart: short fur coat in Kolinsky available in Bond Street. Advertisement in *Harper's Bazaar,* November 1936.

'Morning mist', a typical English country tweed suit in dark autumnal overcheck with cashmere scarf from Fortnum & Mason. Advertisement, October 1936.

Robert Piguet: the 'masculine' cut spring suit in black faille with white dots. *Bernard:* printed crêpe de chine suit with draped and quilted collar and cuffs. Photographs by Dorvyne for *Très Parisien,* spring 1937.

The RETURN OF SEX APPEAL

1937 to 1939

The fabric mills of the great *couture* houses were still grinding away at the beginning of 1937. Into the hoppers had gone all the resources of the earth and out came amusing and imaginative motifs and new-style weaves by the bale. Some new impulse of energy seems to have uncorked fashion's gaiety and recharged the fabric designer's creativity. It was 'impossible to say that these fabrics were particularly shiny or dull, light or heavy, stiff or soft, transparent, smooth or granulated, for they were all these things in turn according to the use to which they were put.' There were brocades, *failles* and heavy satins for evening dresses, jerseys of silk Albène and rayon for draped dinner dresses; for pleated afternoon dresses chiffon was mainly used; and there were lots of stiff organzas, cellophane novelty fabrics, cirés, cloques, taffetas, and an amazing series of new metallic lamés shown in most collections. That season, silhouettes, as well as fabrics, came in an extraordinary variety of designs, which characterized the new, non-conformist feeling. There were 'shorter skirts and higher hats for day', and 'bouffant skirts and slipping shoulders for evening'. There were narrow sheaths, corseletted bust-to-hip tubular drapery, and witty, light-hearted accessories. But the vital new ingredient was sex appeal. Allure was no longer a question of subtlety: this season's recipe for the really smart woman was to 'strip to the waist, more or less, and then shelter under a cartwheel evening hat.'

In 1937, language, too, underwent a new vogue. If the frock you were wearing was the latest from Schiaparelli, if the car you drove was a Bugatti, if you had had your grandmother's diamonds re-set to suit your new, modern way of life — if, in fact, you followed all the rules for entry into the 'smart set', then it was unlikely that you would still be using terms such as 'ripping' or 'old bean'. Such antique phraseology would have dated you as surely as wearing a cloche hat, living with Art Nouveau furniture, or knowing how to dance the Charleston. The fact was that the 'smart set' was 'quite sold' on American slang. You only had to go to one of their fashionable cocktail parties to be engulfed in a spate of transatlanticisms, which described 'swell guys' as being 'the tops', 'swell gals' as being 'pretty smooth' and the less fortunate as 'sob-stuff' or 'the jerkers'.

Of course, the really wealthy members of the new 'smart set' were international travellers, the equivalent of today's 'jet set'. For some time now it might have been the 'in-thing' to have breakfast in London, lunch in Copenhagen and dinner in Budapest. It was so easy to nip across to Paris to do one's shopping once or twice a week, or to drop in unexpectedly on one's Continental friends for a drink or two. The fashionable way to relax was to take one's holidays by air. One could travel to Calcutta in six days, Singapore in eight, and Sydney in only twelve. During this period there could surely have been few sights more impressive than the take-off of one of the majestic new aircraft. 'The vast structure of shining metal moves majestically across the turf and in seven seconds has risen and is fast disappearing into the horizon.' It was the speed that amazed everyone. One minute the giant bird was there, huge, towering, glittering in the sunlight, and then it was gone, winging its way to distant lands.

During this period of technological advance, the same sort of inventive genius that had created the new passenger aeroplanes was also being put into the design and development of luxury liners, racing cars, speedboats and industrial products of every kind. There was Cunard's *Queen Mary*, Sir Malcolm Campbell's *Blue Bird*, and the racing cars of John Cobb and Captain Eyston; there was the development of the 'Yankee Clipper' and Señor de la Cierr's 'Autogiro'. There were improvements in radio and the

Germaine Lecomte and *France Vrament:* spring suits.
Photographs by Dorvyne for *Très Parisien,* spring 1937.

introduction of television, and the construction of new sky-scrapers in New York and modern buildings by Frank Lloyd Wright and Le Corbusier. Soon to be seen, also, were the ingenious inventions of the 1937 Paris Exhibition, which was to be out-done by the New York World Fair just two years later. The larger motor car had also been developing during this period, and cars were now the perfect example of modern functionalism, 'seeming what they were and doing as well as they looked, with their beauty not belying their performance'. The latest model, parked in Bond Street, Fifth Avenue or the Champs-Elysées, would collect a spellbound crowd even faster than a wedding or a fire. 'Drawn-up in superior silence by the kerb, their sleek, high-strung arrogance is as popular a marvel as was ever invented by man.' For the really wealthy the choice seems to have been between a Hispano-Suiza Grand Tourer or a Rolls-Royce drophead coupé. The more modest purchaser could choose between a four and a half-litre Bentley, the Bugatti six-cylinder Sports Special, a Cabriolet Delahaye, an Alvis Speed Twenty-Five, the Straight Eight super-charged Mercedes Benz, a D8—100 Delage and the new 'ultra-smart' American Cord. It was a matter of personal preference and your place in your bank manager's good books. However, the four and a half-litre Lagonda drophead coupé seems to have been the most popular choice for the younger, fashionable Oxbridge set.

'Not since the Edwardian Period have the clothes been so luxurious,' announced one London headline in the mid-spring. This was perhaps in anticipation of the forthcoming Coronation, now that fashionable society had recovered from the shock of the death of George V and the abdication of his eldest son. While the workmen were hammering away at the stands in the Mall, the machinists in a thousand London workrooms were pressing and seaming, tacking and tucking, gathering, embroidering, working at full steam so that everything would be ready for the May festivities. As Coronation Day approached, jewels began to dominate the London scene. There were diamonds, sapphires, rubies and emeralds, to be worn in the hair, on the wrist, on the ears, on the corsage, and all set in new and fascinating designs. Never before, it seemed, had jewels been so brilliant, gorgeous and dazzling, whilst the romantic-looking dresses by the London *couturiers* were far and away more magnificent than any shown in Paris that season. 'The most exquisite of miraculous handwork is being put into the fabulous creations by Hartnell, Stiebel and Handley-Seymore... the lines are simple, so are the décolletages, to be a foil for parures and tiaras... the best are in silver lamé, hand-beaded all over in pearl feathers or gold leaves.'

In Paris, too, the *couturiers*, spurred on by the Coronation as well as the forthcoming Exhibition, seemed determined to have a gala season. They produced a 'stirring array of evening gowns, more shapely and more deeply décolleté than ever before.' For day wear, the accent was on a simpler silhouette, with all the excitement of this mid-season collection being confined to colour and detail. Jackets were mostly straight and short, and skirts flared from a neat waistline. For detailing, intricate buttons were used, such as Schiaparelli's foxes and rams' heads, snakes and mermaids, Mainbocher's silver clasps, Rochas's open books and Patou's flower-pot designs. Colours were hyacinth, cyclamen, petunia, toast, honey, and lots of rainbow, regimental and awning stripes.

And what to wear for the Coronation itself? The peeresses had their traditional robes and the débutantes their bejewelled gowns. But what of those who were neither being presented nor attending the ceremonial celebrations? 'Flowers marshalled into

rows,' came the answer from one of the leading fashion glossies. 'Dark grounds with white daisies or scarlet poppies are the smartest, printed all over a simply-cut redingote and worn over a plain white dress.' Or you could wear 'a white jacket over a dark dress, with dark gloves and dark hat.'

In the autumn of 1937, fashion's faithful followers were reportedly dazzled by the glitter of sequins which sparkled and shimmered throughout the major cities of Europe and America. 'The evenings are afire with sequins, in colours as vivid as the rainbow... Mainbocher's evening dresses had a scintillating skyrocket of sequins bang across them, whilst Schiaparelli scattered hers in coloured handfuls across her evening jackets... Silk satins also shimmered and shone; lamés and brocades were stiff with glittering gold and silver; whilst at several other houses the novelty fabrics made one think of a Rajah's treasury with a dazzling touch of Ziegfeld.' There were also Velázquez ladies, high-breasted and shapely-hipped, and Mistinguett types, tightly sheathed in supple crêpe. Everything that suggested allure was there: the slinky *femme fatale* gown in black brocade satin by Mainbocher, Schiaparelli's suggestive brassière bodices, Paquin's seductively curved hips, Molyneux's tempting décolletages, Vionnet's sexily sophisticated dinner dresses, Alix's tantalizingly clinging evening gowns, and Lanvin's provocative flesh-coloured tights under transparent tea gowns. 'Away with feminine independence and comradeship! Back to feminine power through charm and allure!' went the message. These collections were the clearest expressions of sex appeal and pure seductiveness seen at any time during the thirties.

Early in 1938, 'collection fever' struck once again. At the time it was likened to an outbreak of influenza, 'a highly contagious malady with epidemics annually, in February and August, with an occasional mild attack in April and November.' The daily press were at the collections in full strength, and they had a field day reporting the 'Hot', 'Hotter', 'Hottest' news, alongside the latest crime wave and the ever-deteriorating international situation. At least they provided some light relief from the increasingly ominous reports about the exploits of Herr Hitler and his Third Reich. During those few breathless days in February 1938 while the new collections were being shown, the daily press competed for the latest fashion news, and the more modest papers publicizing the more exotic designs. We can imagine their readers swaying in the crowded trains homeward bound from work, goggle-eyed, as they read that ermine was to be dyed bright apple green, gazing at sketches of sirens in backless chinchilla brassières and see-through Turkish trousers, with ruffled tulle trains, captioned 'for a quiet evening at home'.

Swing music was also sharing the news that spring, with reports that America had gone 'swing crazy'. In Europe it was daily gaining new devotees; rhythm clubs were being formed, jam sessions were being held and thousands of records were being sold. But it was in America that the famous swing musicians were the most popular. To the stirring rhythms of the swing orchestras, a new kind of dancing was being evolved, compared with which the wildest Charlestons and Black Bottoms of a few years earlier seemed like stately minuets. At swing 'conventions' staged before large audiences, orchestras and dancers let themselves go in a mixture of carefully-planned craziness and violent improvization. New fashions were being worn by the 'jitter-bugs', as the dancers were called, and ten-dollar words were being invented by psychologists to explain the phenomenon. Many people were alarmed at this apparent madness, but, as was pointed out at the time, 'it is better to be living in a land where fun isn't a felony, where a "killer-diller" is a hot swing artist and not a poison gas expert, and where the tap-tap of the jitter-bug's shoes is sweet music compared to the martialled tramp of countless jackbooted feet as they goose-step along the path of death and destruction.'

While the year of 1938 witnessed a succession of world-shattering events, coquetry was making its return to the world of high fashion, and the reign of artifice was revived with the re-introduction of the corset. These corsets were entirely different, however, from the agonizing affairs worn during the Victorian era. They were soft and comfortable, made of fine cotton, long and boned in the front, ending a couple of inches below the waist at the sides and laced at the back for personal adjustment. They were curved and cut to support and shape the figure, giving a high-busted, spare-rib look for the new fashionable Winterhalter dresses.

This new, romantic-looking silhouette was widely publicized in all the international glossy magazines of the period, including *La Femme Chic, Harper's Bazaar, Vogue, Femina* and *L'Officiel,* and illustrated by the leading photographers Hoynigen-Huène, Horst, Man Ray, Cecil Beaton, Georges Saad, Louise Dahl-Wolfe and Norman Parkinson, all of whom conveyed in their individual ways the latest ideal of feminine beauty. Other designs were illustrated by the drawings of such distinguished artists as Carl Ericsson, René Bouet Willaumez, René Bouché, Christian Bérard, Vertès and Pierre Mourgue, whose skilful lines captured the spirit of the new mode. For the first time, too, these fashions were being illustrated by 'word pictures' which were broadcast direct from Paris to New York while the clothes were still being shown.

For day wear, the 'Up, Up, Up Fashion' was the rage. Hats went up, hair went up, collars went up, skirts went up — and of course, prices went up. This last led a number of journalists to complain about the exorbitant cost of *couture* dresses, though others explained that at £20 for a simple day dress and £80 for an elaborate evening dress, prices really hadn't changed since the beginning of the decade. 'No one is paying for a handsome label, the depression has seen to that. They pay the price knowing that they have bought the very best available.' That season, fourteen yards of brocade were used in one grand evening dress, and ten yards of silk lamé, specially woven in Lyons, in a cocktail suit. Eight women worked for six days on a single lace evening gown. A tailor worked thirty-six hours putting together a wool suit, whilst a seamstress took forty hours to make a dance dress from narrow bands of tucked net. 'One girl works for three days on a scrap of a hat, a shoemaker carries out one hundred and sixty different operations on a pair of shoes, and six hundred silver paillettes are sewn on by hand for an evening belt. This,' it was explained, 'is what makes fashion expensive.' But the smartest women were 'willing to pay the price because they know that whatever they order will be the best of its kind in the world.'

In the spring of 1939 hats represented the pinnacle of fashion, 'the high spot of smartness, the crown of femininity, that last touch of mystery which is designed to stir the actress in you and whirl you into a springtime mood, regardless of the European Situation.' These were hats 'that other women always talk about but which they would never have the courage to wear. Hats that seek, brazenly, that hard-hearted chic, that direct, deliberate, stark, slick chic which has been missing from fashion since the beginning of the decade.'

Hats were only the beginning of the changes that were to take place in fashion in 1939. The great *couturiers* lifted from the crackling tissue of their spring bandboxes a new batch of fabrics in new colours and interesting weaves, and a whole new crop of day and afternoon frocks, dresses, suits and coats. They had also been refining the high-busted silhouette for evening wear, 'slimming the figure around the waist and adding a little more shape to the bust and hips so that they are softly curved, in all those places where tradition says women are most alluring.' In response to this new fashion trend, the waists of fashionable women had to become slimmer than those of the 'streamlined Amazons' of the early 1930s. 'Diet, if you need, exercise if you must, but to wear the new clothes you need the new corsets, for the corset is the clue to the new silhouette.' Women were advised to look at themselves in a full-length mirror. 'Have you ever thought what a dreary world it would be if we all went about with the face, the hair and the body shape that God gave us? Today it is just as uncivilized to go out without a certain amount of make-up as it will be tomorrow to go out without the new, shapely corset.'

Apart from the endless discussions about the worsening international situation, the talk at social gatherings throughout the summer in London, Paris and New York continued to revolve around the new slimmer waistline and more feminine curves. The autumn collections of the great dressmakers confirmed this new silhouette, with designs calling for even more uplift and a tighter wasp-waist. 'The new dresses demand it, corsets contrive it', was the new fashion slogan. Not since the days of the Victorian eighteen-inch waist had fashion been so corset-conscious. Those vague terms 'support' and 'control', generally associated with advertisements directed at the middle-aged, were replaced by new, definite demands for a 'ring-sized waist', a 'long, smooth, stemlike torso', and 'bosoms which are definitely bosom-shaped'. All of this could be achieved by 'modern magic' with corsets which were 'as persuasive as a whisper', capable of coaxing two inches off the waist and adding them to the bust, transforming the wearer without her even being conscious of wearing them. As if to emphasize the sleekness of the new feminine figure, several Parisian *couturiers*, notably the French designer Alix, the American Mainbocher, the Italian Schiaparelli, the Englishman Molyneux and the Spaniard Balenciaga, added a bustle at the back of many of their evening dresses. Far from the old-fashioned, Victorian blacksmith's contrivance, these bustles consisted of 'a substantial drape of material at the back of a number of the new dresses', whilst other dresses had 'an extra fold of material looped over at the back, or tied into a bow to give the fashionable bustle effect'. On the third of September 1939, the threatened holocaust in Europe became an imminent reality with the official declaration of war. Late in October of that fateful year, all the great *couturiers* assembled, with all the glory and grandeur that they could muster, the last fashion shows of the decade. 'Suspense has attended the creation of these dresses,' it was declared. 'They are dramatic because in drama they were made. They were born in crisis and launched in war.' Indeed, they verify well the historian's theory, that the more serious the times, the more triumphantly fashion asserts itself. These new mid-winter fashions, with their flared skirts and close-fitting jackets were reported by the major newspapers and magazines of the free world as being 'in the full glamorous tradition of fashion with elegant and exquisite designs'. But for the majority of women, it all seemed to have lost its former importance. For the next seven years, the fashions already in use were to remain unaltered, and it was not until after the war, when the

Reboux: black straw auréole hat, ribboned and bowed in red and violet. Photograph by Joffé for *Femina,* March 1938.

Mainbocher: black cocktail dress. Veiled toque by *Suzanne Talbot.* Photograph by Joffé for *Femina,* March **1938**.

austerity regulations had been lifted, that the 'new look' designs of 1939 could be seen and assessed by the general public.

During the first few days of the war a new, utilitarian fashion had emerged. Women were putting on uniforms, boiler suits or jumpers and skirts, and of course, tin hats. They had decided that the time had come to work alongside the men in the armed forces or factories. For a while it seemed as if the most feminine of their instincts had gone into hiding as they continued to channel their energies into the war effort. Even in their time off, women seemed content to tuck their hair into a crocheted snood, and to put on a 'made over' blouse, a newly shortened skirt and thicker stockings.

At last, in 1947, the very feminine New Look fashions shown in the Paris Spring collections hit the headlines, and the name of Christian Dior was on everybody's lips. Perhaps it would be an over-simplification to say that the Dior New Look designs of 1947 were exactly the same as the 'new look' designs of 1939. But the similarity was there, in the high, rounded bust-line, the wasp-waist and the padded hips. Fashion never waits, not even for a war; even so, I cannot help but wonder how those designs might have developed had the war not intervened in September 1939. But that's another story, to be told in another book.

Chanel: cocktail dress in Chantilly lace with paillettes. 'Coiffure de plumes' by *Collier.* Photograph by Georges Saad, September 1938.

Maggy Rouff: autumn fashions in black satin with white lace and tulle cuffs and matching silver fox. Pear-drop necklace, felt hat and toque by *Agnès.* Photograph by Joffé, October 1938.

Hermès: blue and white tailored ottoman summer suit and white embroidered linen dress. Advertisement, June 1938.

Kent and Frances: stranded lynx coat. Advertisement, October 1938.

Balenciaga: pink and silver moiré dress, with pink uncurled ostrich boa (left); heavy white satin dress, incrusted and tasselled with absinthe-yellow velvet (right). Photograph by Hoyningen-Huène for *Harper's Bazaar,* October 1938.

Classic Burberry travel coat and matching suit in English tweed. Advertisement, November 1938.

Marcelle Dormoy and *Nina Ricci:* **green and white satin** blouses for a Christmas 'at home'. Photograph by Joffé, December 1938.

COIFFURES ET PIERRERIES

Callot and *Georgius:* evening hair styles for the Christmas season. Photographs by Dax, December 1938.

Patou: silk moiré dress and jacket from the spring collection of 1939. Photograph by Jean Moral for *Harper's Bazaar*, April 1939.

Matita: brown top coat for the new under-the-hour cross-Channel trip to France. Advertisement, August 1939.

Schiaparelli: white mackintosh. Photograph by Jean Moral during the first few days of the Second World War, in Paris, for *Harper's Bazaar,* October 1939.

Dinner dress for the first Christmas of the Second World War. Advertisement, December 1939.

It's a "Tested-Quality" Fabric

MADE WITH

Courtaulds

RAYON

You'll still be "going places" this Xmas! Here is the ideal dinner dress (with new, short skirt) the bodice of lace, embroidered with sequins . . .

Molyneux: pale grey chiffon evening dress. Photograph by Ermin Blumenfeld, in Paris, for the last fashion magazine of the decade *Harper's Bazaar*, December 1939.